Discovering GOD'S Purpose

Dr. D. K. Olukoya

Discovering God's
PURPOSE

Dr. D. K. Olukoya

Discovering God's PURPOSE

© 2012 Dr. D. K. Olukoya

Published - December, 2012

ISBN : 978-978-920-053-5

Published by:
The Battle Cry Christian Ministries
322, Herbert Macaulay Way, Yaba,
P. O. Box 12272, Ikeja, Lagos State, Nigeria.
Phone: 01 8044415, 0803 304 4239,
e-mail: info@battlecrystore.com
customercare@battlecrystore.com
sales@battlecrystore.com
website: www.battlecrystore.com

I salute my wonderful wife, Pastor Shade, for her invaluable support in the ministry. I appreciate her unquantifiable support in the book Ministry as the cover designer, art editor and art adviser.

All the Scriptures are from the King James Version

Cover Illustration : Pastor (Mrs.) Shade Olukoya

All rights reserved. No part of this publication may be reproduced, stored in a retrieval system, or transmitted in any form or by any means, electronic, mechanical, photocopying, recording or otherwise without the prior written permission of the publishers.

Printed in Nigeria.

Table of Contents

CHAPTER	PAGE
1. DISCOVERING GOD'S PURPOSE	4
2. HINTS ON SUCCESS	19
3. FULFILLING YOUR DESTINY	29
4. WHEN YOU WIN	44

CHAPTER 1
Discovering God's PURPOSE

God has a purpose for each of us, so you must strive to know who you are otherwise you might be opening your door to problems. The question of identity is an important one. Jacob learnt that lesson; he knew that by his identity he was not in his place of blessing. If you recall from your study of the Bible, Jacob used foul means to usurp his brother's blessing. He used the expedient of impersonation to achieve his purpose although this looks reprehensible from the human point of view.

Let this be clear in your spirit that, one of Satan's most effective devices is to get people to doubt their identity. He did it to Jesus, he said that if He was the Son of God, He should command stones to become bread. He did not stop at that. Again he told Jesus that if He was the Son of God He should cast Himself down. And when Jesus was on the cross, Satan came again to tempt Him. He told Jesus that if He was truly the son of God, He should come down from the cross. It is therefore possible for the devil to challenge you by saying that if you are truly a child of God you should not be suffering.

THE IMPORTANT QUESTION

It is wise for you to know the answer to the important question, **"who are you?** That is why, as a believer, you should not confess negatively. For example, don't say, **"I am not worthy" "I am worn out," "I am unfit"** etc. That

Discovering God's PURPOSE

was your old identity tag, but once you have given your life to Jesus and if, by the grace of God, you are living the kind of life God wants you to live, you should not call yourself strange names again. But if you still do, it means you don't know who you are.

The prodigal son was rotten and bad but at a stage he came back to his senses and remembered who he was; he remembered that he was a son and not a slave. So you too must remember who you are. When Jesus was in the world, he did not hide his identity. He identified himself as "**the Light,**" and "**the bread of life.**" The Bible tells us what our identity is. It says .that we are "**the branches,**" "**new creatures,**" not refurbished ones. The Bible says we are "**God's workmanship,**" "**we are more than conquerors,**" and our lives are hid in Christ. All these point to our collective identity and you must know them.

Do not be like Peter who was released from jail and did not know because he was surprised. The day you know that you belong to God, your creator, that day you will begin a victorious life. At this juncture, I like you to pray this way,
1. **O Lord show me who I am in the spirit, in Jesus' name.**
2. **O Lord open my understanding in the name of Jesus."**
It was possible for Elijah to do exploits for the Lord because he realized his position in the Lord, he knew his identity early enough. Who are you then in the spiritual scale of the

Almighty God? What can you use to identify yourself in the spirit? Please pray again that the garment of ignorance should be roasted in the name of Jesus.

WHERE ARE YOU?

> And the Lord God called unto Adam, and said unto him, Where art thou? And he said, I heard thy voice in the garden, and I was afraid, because I was naked; and I hid myself – Genesis 3:9-10.

In contemporary English, the question becomes, **"where are you?"** What an interesting question! Was it that God did not know where Adam was? The question was asked because Adam was no longer in the right place, he had left where God wanted him to be. Because Adam was in the wrong place, God changed his original intention for him. He threw Him out of the garden and put an angel with the sword of fire at the gate so that the man would not find his way back there.

Know this beloved, that when you depart from the path of God for your life, a forty days' journey will take forty years. It is a pity that so many people have never really found out God's plan for their lives or have abandoned the plan after listening to people of the world. I do hope you know that education and material possessions are not signs that you are enjoying God's blessings. The sign can only be seen in you when you are at the center of God's will.

Are you at the center of God's will for your life? Or are you like David who stayed at home while others were fighting (remember Bathsheba, Uriah's wife?) or Peter who stayed in the wrong place? No wonder then that Peter at a point started to follow God from afar. Are you in the wrong place in your career, business, or spiritual life? When you are in the wrong place you cannot receive God's blessings. All that you can get are crumbs here and there. You will not be in proper fellowship with the Lord and this will make you an easy target for the devil. When the question is posed, **"where are you?"** the meaning is, where is your spiritual location in God? What do you weigh in His balance?

Nebuchadnezzar was a very great king and there had never been a kingdom so great in splendour and might and glory like the Kingdom of Babylon he ruled. But God dealt with him when he got too proud. God sent him into the bush and humiliated him completely; he ate leaves like animals. Whatever you are doing whether good or bad, God has His weighing balance. So if God were to put you in His scale at this moment, where you are will determine your weight on the scale.

ZERO WEIGHT

A lot of people's weight is just zero. Ask yourself: "**where am I in the spiritual scale of the Almighty?**" If you love yourself say "**I refuse to be used as a bad example in the name of Jesus**". When you are not where you should be, you can become an easy target for the enemy.

What is your spiritual temperature? Perhaps the Lord has searched for you amongst divine dreamers, visioners, prophets etc and your name was not in any of these classes. Then suddenly the devil shouts saying, "**God, I have his name in my evil books! I have her name in my terrible records**". So the voice of the Lord is ringing out to you today loud and clear saying, "**Where are you?**"

A lot of spiritually lame people go to church. Their gift of vision has disappeared. They used to be on fire but now they have become cold. We have spiritually deaf and dumb people too in large numbers in many churches today. They do not hear from the Lord neither do they see any vision. They do not comprehend anything. It is not surprising at all, that such people invest even in wrong places in the secular or business world. Your answer to this question is very important, "**Where are you?**" Belteshazzar eventually knew where he was. God showed him that he was through with computing the worth of his administration, He had weighed it and found it wanting.

Discovering God's PURPOSE

Please close your eyes and talk to the Lord about yourself this way: "**Set my life on fire for You and bury all my lukewarmness in the name of Jesus.**" Looking inward, are you still being harassed by the spirit of fear? If the kind of things that used to put your heart on the race is still doing so now, it shows that you have not grown at all. Perhaps your faith is still as rudimentary as when you just believed.

Perhaps your knowledge of God is so hazy that you have never used the name of Jesus to defeat any power of the enemy in your life. Perhaps you have been a believer for one year or two and you cannot differentiate between the voice of the Holy Spirit, your voice and the devil's. The solution is to seek help and not to console yourself by saying that you are better than someone else.

Most people have not bothered to ask themselves where they came from. Have you ever thought of that? Where is your origin? Although this is important, many people nonetheless do not think of their roots, that is, where they came from. It is certain that somebody, who does not know where he is coming from, would not know where he is heading for.

YOUR DESTINATION

If, for instance, you don't know why you are a Christian, you will not know what you want in this life and hereafter.

If your answer to the question, "**Where do you come from,**" is "**I don't know,**" that is quite unsatisfactory. You must know your origin. The Bible makes it crystal clear that God created you and me. It has this to say:

> *What is man, that thou art mindful of him? and the son of man, that thou visitest him? For thou hast made him a little lower than the angels, and hast crowned him with glory and honour. Thou madest him to have dominion over the works of thy hands; thou hast put all things under his feet* — Psalm 8:4-6.

This tells us that man was created by God, but a time came when man lost all the glory of God and man got into trouble. So no matter how great a man is, his physical body is dust. The Lord told him, "**dust thou art and unto the dust thou shalt return.**" It is only the spirit of man that goes back to God. So, the next time you feel like boasting, remember "**dust thou art and unto the dust thou shalt return.**" Let it be very clear in your spirit, that whether a person is rich or poor unto the dust shall he or she return. We came from God and to Him shall we return at the expiration of our time.

YOUR FUTURE

The Bible answers the question. The Bible paints the picture of two places and the contrast between them is frightening. The world we are in now is Satan's. The kingdom of God will come and overcome this one. Jesus said clearly that when men die they go to either of two places: heaven or hell fire. The Bible's graphic description of these two places makes the contrast very clear. It is given to man to die only once after that judgement and it is better for a person not to be born at all than to end up in hell fire. The Bible makes us realize that when the rich man died, he found himself in hell fire; Lazarus too died but found himself in the bosom of Abraham. Talk to the Lord in prayers like this: **"Anything that will take me to hell fire, get out of my life now, in the name of Jesus"**

God is interested in our total life. He is interested in how well we are doing. Do you know the biblical truth that a thousand years in His sight is like a passing night? God has His own arithmetic. The question is, what do you weigh in His balance? How are you on His spiritual scale now? Are you a **"thermostat Christian,"** the type that the environment determines his temperature?

What God needs first is our spirit man. The fire that has entered the spirit is sufficient to melt all problems away. How can fire enter into the spirit when the spirit is already blocked? What adjustment has God been asking you to make in your life? Has He been asking you to correct your thinking, dressing, speech, prayer life or Bible reading?

YOUR VISION

Let us go to the book of Jeremiah. The Lord asked Jeremiah an interesting question.

> Then the Lord said unto me, Out of the north an evil shall break forth upon all the inhabitants of the land. Then the word of the Lord came unto me, saying, Before I formed thee in the belly I knew thee; and before thou camest forth out of the womb I sanctified thee, and I ordained thee a prophet unto the nations. Then said I, Ah, Lord God! behold, I cannot speak: for I am a child. But the Lord said unto me, Say not, I am a child: for thou shalt go to all that I shall send thee, and whatsoever I command thee thou shalt speak. Be not afraid of their faces: for I am with thee to deliver thee, saith the Lord. Then the Lord put forth his hand, and touched my mouth. And the Lord said unto me, Behold, I have put my words in thy mouth. See, I have this day set thee over the nations and over the kingdoms, to

Discovering God's PURPOSE

> *root out, and to pull down, and to destroy, and to throw down, to build, and to plant. Moreover the word of the Lord came unto me, saying, Jeremiah, what seest thou? And I said, I see a rod of an almond tree. Then said the Lord unto me, Thou hast well seen: for I will hasten my word to perform it. And the word of the Lord came unto me the second time, saying, "What seest thou? And I said, I see a seething pot; and the face thereof is toward the north. Then the Lord said unto me, Out of the north an evil shall break forth upon all the inhabitants of the land* — Jeremiah 1:4-14.

So I ask you the same question, **"what do you see?"** Was it that the Lord did not know what Jeremiah saw? Why did he ask that question? The Lord may be showing you the vision for your life and you may not see it. Your spiritual vision may have what can be called **"spiritual cataract,"** which can prevent you from seeing what the Lord wants you to see. If you have made up your mind on what you want to do and then approach the Lord saying, **"O Lord show me the way,"** you can be sure that you will not see anything, for you have already made up your mind on what to do before coming to the Lord.

GOD'S UNIQUE PURPOSE

Beloved, perhaps you are without a vision or plan for your Christian life, you really need to pray. The voice of the Lord is asking you, **"what do you see?"** God never calls a meeting for entertainment. At the Mountain of Fire and Miracles Ministries for example, there is no room for satanic entertainment. There is quite a number of glitzy churches all around for those searching for entertainment. God has a serious purpose for bringing people to fellowship at MFM.

God has His serious purposes. Even if the whole world is aimless and purposeless, God has a purpose for everything he does. God believes in man so much that He invested so much in him by sending His son to die and He expects returns from man. If I may ask you this question, **"do you know for sure what is happening to you?"** What stage are you in the history of your life?

Have you seen the personal vision God has for you? Do you know your purpose in life? If you don't know the vision of God for your life, then you will not be able to plan. God does not experiment, for He knows what He is doing, so the earlier you find out what He wants you to do and you begin to do it, the better. God is called the Alpha and the Omega because before He starts a thing He has completed it.

Discovering God's PURPOSE

God never starts a thing without finishing it. God determined that Jesus was to be born and that he would die to redeem man. All these were clear in His mind before he started to look for Mary to bring forth the child. Why did God allow your birth? Don't be one of those people getting confused or prospering in the wrong times. The fact that what you are doing prospers does not mean that it is right. Please close your eyes and pray seriously to the Lord this way **"Open my eyes to see your purpose for my life in the name of Jesus"**.

THE YARDSTICK

Now there are two ways to recognize those people who don't have visions for their lives. They prophesy and disobey the prophecy; they report hearing the Lord say, **"my servant, my servant, I want to use you mightily."** But curiously enough, the same person, who heard the voice of the Lord, still commits sin indiscriminately around. People always move from one business to the other without making a headway; they don't really know what God wants them to do. They choose their spouses on the basis of physical attributes. They receive direct messages from the Lord and then throw them aside. They want to lead others but they don't want to be led. And when minor failures crop up they get discouraged. These are the people without visions.

But for somebody who knows what he has seen, all the discouragement and failures on the way are nothing but fertilizers. Those without vision are the ones who see men looking like trees. They criticize others concerning sins which they themselves commit. They don't know whether they are hearing from God or the devil. There are many of them in the churches agitating for church posts. Some find it difficult to serve the Lord unless they are in a Leadership positions.

Many of us often dream but how many of us know what we are dreaming about? Have you got to that level where when you have a puzzling dream, you are able to ask for its meaning from the Lord right away, or do you wake up still confused and seeking to fathom the dream for the next three months? No, you need to move past this level.

Rise up today and do what the Lord wants you to do. Do not behave like a hypocrite because the hopes of the hypocrites shall perish. If the trumpet shall utter an uncertain sound, the Bible says, who shall prepare for battle? What kind of fruit is your life producing? Are they positive that will attract people to the Lord or are they fruits that will lead people down to the bottom of hell fire? You are going to open your mouth and pray aggressively the following prayer points with your right hand on your chest.

PRAYER POINTS

1. I refuse to let sin have dominion over me, in the name of Jesus.

2. I bind you, the spirit of anger, in the name of Jesus.

3. I bind you, the spirit of lying, in the name of Jesus.

4. I bind you, the spirit of worrying, in the name of Jesus.

5. Lord, come into my heart in a different way, in the name of Jesus.

6. Every tree of spiritual failure be uprooted, in the name of Jesus.

CHAPTER 2

Hints On SUCCESS

Discovering God's PURPOSE

When a question or a matter is referred to as a "**secret**," it means such is never available in the public domain. It means it is not everybody that can have access to it. It is not everybody that has knowledge of the thing called a "**secret**." Someone may look at a thing that makes another thing larger and more complex work without really grasping an understanding of its mechanism. You might meet an angel or the personality of the Holy Spirit without taking the fact in. Men could be very ignorant of spiritual things. What are the secrets which the Apostles concentrated upon?

1. **THE HOLY SPIRIT WAS EMPHASISED IN THE MINISTRY OF THE APOSTLES :** The evangelical endeavour and the wonders wrought by the Apostles were facilitated by the Holy Spirit. The will of the Lord is that you should be filled with the Holy Spirit so that everything you do will be done under His auspices. The book of Acts says that the Holy Spirit came upon Peter and he opened his mouth. Peter was preaching and teaching by the power of the Holy Spirit. He was not using his human reasoning and wisdom. If the church of God today could seek the in filling of the Spirit with all holiness and vehemence, it would be the beginning of a great revival and the explosion of God's power in our midst. Paul too was filled with the Holy Ghost which enabled him to speak so boldly. Most of

our utterances, teaching, preaching carry little or no fire because of lack of the in filling of the Holy Spirit. The lack of power, grace and glory in the church today is due to the dilution of the teaching of the Holy Spirit with human theology. The ignorance of the modern-day Christianity is so pronounced to the extent that anyone who is truly filled with the Holy Spirit is accused of operating under demonic influence.

2. **EMPHASIS ON THE CHURCHES IN THE HOUSE RATHER THAN ON CHURCH BUILDING:** The house fellowship structure of the Apostles of those days was very strong. Many Christians today are not bothered about house fellowship because they do not know that it is the secret of church growth. There are those who believe that they are too versed in the word or too dignified socially to be seen interacting with the dregs in a dingy apartment in the neighbourhood. House fellowship is God's way of spreading His fire across the land. House fellowship is the quickest way of possessing our environment for God. If the church comes under persecution the only mechanism left for member to meet is the house fellowship forum.

3. **THE APOSTLES EMPHASISED YOKE BREAKING BY THE ANOINTING.**

4. **THEY REGARDED THEMSELVES AS A SINGLE UNIT**: They were bound together in love. There was no division or schism among them. That was why God was able to bless them mightily.

5. **THEY PRAYED POWERFUL PRAYERS:** The Bible says that when the apostles gathered together, the place they were praying was shaken. They prayed powerful prayers.

Raise your right hand and pray thus: "**Every conspiracy in the heavenlies against my destiny, scatter, in the name of Jesus.**"

An understanding of church history will reveal that few years after the crucifixion of our Lord Jesus Christ, the disciples spread Christianity all over the then known world.

In spite of persecution by Emperor Nero and the endemic atmosphere of hostility to the gospel in the Roman empire, half of the citizens of the empire became secret disciples of Christ, albert crypto-Christians.

THE GREAT CHASM

These men (disciples), although were not educated as many of us are now, they turned the whole world upside down. It then appears that there are certain things those disciples knew which we do not know as regards the issues of the kingdom. They were walking in a realm that the present day crop of believers are ignorant of.

The disciples attained that height with little or no communication technology as we have it today. They did not even have the printed Bibles in their hands.

In spite of the advantages that the modern-day Christians have from the radio, television, recording, printing and publications, traveling and education, yet they have accomplished far less than the apostles brought out within a few years. Could it be that the first church knew certain secrets which the present-day believers do not know?

A close examination of their messages show that we are preaching the same messages they preached but the impact they made is far greater than the impact made by the modern day church. Why is this so?

THE LORD IS DEMANDING BOTH THE FIRSTBORN AND THE FIRST FRUITS: This is another secret that the Apostles had. Look at Exodus 22:29.

> *Thou shalt not delay to offer the first of thy ripe fruits, and of thy liquors: the firstborn of thy sons shalt thou give unto me.*

Discovering God's PURPOSE

Here the Lord is asking for the first-born and the first fruits.

Why is God asking for the first born and the first fruits?

Let us get the answer from Genesis 49: 3.

> *Reuben, thou art my firstborn, my might, and the beginning of my strength, the excellency of dignity, and the excellency of power.*

This statement was made by Jacob when he held his famous farewell benediction cum prediction session with his twelve children. Consider the implication of the primacy of the firstborn in the foregoing verse: *my might, beginning of my strength, excellency of dignity and excellency of power.*

Unfortunately, there are first children in many families who are not finding their feet. There are so many a firstborn whose lifestyle is like that of the lastborn. God Himself adopted Israel as His firstborn.

God's firstborn (Israel) were once in Egypt. God demanded that His Firstborn should be released but Pharaoh refused. Pharaoh had no option but to release them by the time God dealt with all the Firstborn in Egypt.

FIRSTBORN DEDICATION

The lesson drawn from the issue of firstborn is that whatsoever is first belongs to God because God is the first.

There would always be trouble for any firstborn dedicated to any other "**god**" or thing expect God. Once a firstborn is not dedicated to God there is a serious battle for such. Jesus also is God's firstborn. God needs the firstborn.

Just as God is much interested in the human firstborn, He is also much interested in the firstborn of every product.

Take Cain and Abel for example. Cain failed but Abel succeeded. There was Ishmael and Isaac. Isaac was chosen but Ishmael was not. Another was Esau and Jacob. Esau was the firstborn but he was not chosen. Another example is Reuben and Joseph. Reuben was the firstborn but he was not chosen. There was Manasseh and Ephraim. Manasseh was the firstborn but he was not chosen. There was Aaron and Moses. Aaron the elder was not chosen but Moses. There was the brothers of David in the Bible. Eliab was the most senior but He was not chosen. David was chosen in place of Eliab.

THE PLIGHT OF THE FIRSTBORN

A careful student of the Bible would have noted that it is silent about the mother of David. It is being opined that he might have been born by a woman different from the mother of his brethren. All the brothers of David were old enough to have him as a son. When Jesse was eventually asked to bring all his sons, he did not even count David as a prospective somebody much less a potential monarch. David was not regarded because he was quite small. And still, Eliab failed but David succeeded.

There is another man called Adonijah. Adonijah, the first child, was not chosen as the king but Solomon. Almost all the firstborn from Genesis to Malachi ended up being failures. It looks difficult finding the firstborn who really pleased God.

Remember that Noah was not the firstborn; Joseph was not the firstborn neither was David.

The truth of the matter is that, the devil hates all the firstborns with a perfect hatred and he fights them hard. Immediately the devil knew that there was a good prophecy about Judah the first thing he did was to kill his firstborn mysteriously.

Jesus was the true firstborn that looked at the devil eye to eye and dealt with him. It was from the book of Genesis that the devil gathered that Jesus, as the true firstborn, would deal with him. That was why satan started to fight every firstborn in the fear of the coming Messiah who should bruise his head.

If the firstborn is not dedicated to the Lord, the problem in his life would increase. The early Christians understood this point. They understood the principles behind the success or failure of the firstborn.

In the practice of firstfruit offering, it is advisable that when you get your first salary which is the firstborn of your labour, do not touch it, do not spend it but bring it to God's house. If you do that, then your promotion would be very rapid. Special favour would be your portion. I remember that the principle of first fruit prompted me to give out my first salary to God. I took it to the pastor straight. And the pastor prayed for me from the depth of his heart as a result of my obedience to God's instruction. This obedience had seen me through several hurdles of life. I received favour anywhere I worked from that time. You might ask, **"How would I drop my whole salary to God?"** But what would happen if God did not provide the work in the first instance?

Prayer Points
1. Let every failure in the dream be converted to success, in the name of Jesus.
2. I nullify all curses of failure in my life, in Jesus' name.
3. I pull down every stronghold of failure in my life, in the name of Jesus.

4. I pull down every stronghold of failure in my marriage, in the name of Jesus.
5. I pull down every stronghold of failure in my business, in the name of Jesus.
6. Every pipeline of failure connected to my life, I command you to receive the fire of God and be consumed, in Jesus' name.
7. Every spiritual barrier to success in my life, I command you to break into pieces, in Jesus' name.
8. Every inherited and self-inflicted failure in my life, I command you to reversed, in the name of Jesus.
6. Every seed of failure in my life, I command you to be consumed by the fire of God, in the name of Jesus.
9. Every area of my life lost to failure, I command you to be restored, in Jesus' name.
10. Every area of my life lost to failure, I command you to be restored, in Jesus' name.
11. You spirit of failure, loose your grip over my life, in Jesus' name.
12. I refuse to register in the school of failure, in the mighty name of Jesus.
13. Lord, let me not enter the trap of failure, in the name of Jesus.
14. I remove my name from the book of failure and demonic sidetrack, in the name of Jesus.

CHAPTER 3

Fulfilling Your DESTINY

Discovering God's PURPOSE

Ecclesiastes 10:7 make this thought-provoking statement:

> *I have seen servants upon horses, and princes walking as servants upon the earth.*

Your destiny is the inner purpose of your life. You can have an outer purpose for life. The inner one, the real reason why you are breathing and going up and down is what you call your destiny. Your destiny is a condition foreordained by God for you. In that passage, we see a man who has been ordained as a prince but has become a servant. He was pre-ordained to be a prince. Your destiny is the purpose of God for your life. Your destiny is the plan and programme of God for your life. He did not send you here to be messing about. He did not send you here not to know what you are doing or to be floating all over the place.

Your destiny is what you are really meant for. Your destiny is what you have been called to be and to do. Your destiny is why you were born or the expectations of heaven for your life. What does heaven expect you to do here? Does heaven just want you to come, get married if it is possible, get certificates, have children and at the end of the day you die? Would that be all that the heavens want you to come and do here? Your destiny is what is written in heavenly records concerning you. Your destiny is what God had in mind, the original intention of God before He created you and sent you down here.

The greatest tragedy of mankind happens when people don't move in their divine destiny, when people don't move the way God wants them to move, when they don't sit where God wants them to sit, or stand where God wants them to stand. They want to be copycats and that is leading them to a limitation. It is indeed a tragedy.

Ecclesiastes chapter 10 verse 7 quoted above hints upon a disturbing skewing or perversion of destiny. Unfortunately, this is the lot of many people who are living on earth. This verse is pregnant with meanings but the bottom line of what it is saying is that, many are not where they are supposed to be. Servants have taken over the horses of princes and princes are walking as servants upon the earth; destiny vultures.

Destiny means to determine something beforehand. So, your destiny is what God has pre-ordained for your future.

BLIND FOLKS

There are many blind people here on earth. Some are floating around. Some don't know what they are doing, and many are students in the school of witchcraft manipulation. Many people have been diverted by the powers of darkness. Some have diverted themselves. Some are unconsciously diverted, some have consciously diverted themselves. Some are consciously diverted. The bottom line is that majority of men and women living on the surface of the earth don't really know who they are and where they are going. It is a very tragic thing. This is why I would like you to raise up your voice and pray for yourself like this: **"Any power, firing arrow of confusion into my spirit, die, in the name of Jesus."**

Your life is like a book and you write a chapter each day. What you write would eventually be read on the Day of Judgment. The question is, what are you writing about your life? The Bible says, **"If the trumpet shall give an uncertain sound, who shall prepare for battle?"** The question is, what kind of sound will the trumpet of your life give?

Many people married their enemies as husbands. Some married serpents as wives. Some married cockroaches, lions, etc. As each man is missing the way and doing the wrong thing, there is a regular spiritual accident taking place in the spirit world thereby confusing man the most. Also, there is a power behind all these things which laughs men of God to scorn.

WHAT IS A VULTURE?

A vulture is a large bird of prey. It does not even kill other birds or other animals; it preys on those which are dead. It feeds on the flesh of dead animals. It is a bird most people do not want to see. It is not beautiful at all. It is very ugly.

In fact, the major part of its neck and head do not have feathers. It is a horrible thing to see a vulture in your dream. If you see a vulture in your dream, the deep thing that is being revealed to you is that you are just a corpse walking about.

Vultures can smell death. They are naturally endowed with the ability to know when somebody is about to die. In times of war, you see vultures waiting patiently for dying soldiers to give up so that they can swoop on them. This is why it is often said that the vulture is a patient bird. The vulture has a very sharp sight like the eagle. It can smell the almost-dead person and then wait for him to die. There are thousands of spiritual vultures waiting to feed or are feeding on the flesh of many destinies.

Physical animals have spiritual counterparts and each of them in the spirit means something completely different. The vulture is one of the unclean animals the Bible says we should not eat. The vulture that ate up the destiny of Esau was an ordinary bowl of food and that is still happening now. The vulture that eats up the destiny of some people is comfort. The one that ate up the destiny of some people is discouragement. There are no rewards for trying. There are only rewards for finishing. If you give up in the middle of a race even though you were in the front when you stopped, you get nothing. Another vulture that is eating the destiny of some people is deception.

It is sad but true, that there are people who have experienced the move of the power of God in their lives before but now that is history. I used to know a brother in those days, who was so gifted in the things of the Spirit that he could understand the language of birds. But very soon it became a thing of the past in his life. It was so terrible that if human beings were talking, he found it difficult to understand. Many have taken sabbatical leave from the presence of the Lord. And for some, talking to God is like talking to a brick wall. Such people should know that destiny vultures are after them and if they allow them to catch up, it will be very sad.

DIVERSE DREAMS

When you see yourself naked in a dream, that is a serious matter. Similarly, when you are pursued in your dream, that also should not be shrugged off. A person that is being pursued cannot concentrate. He cannot be settled. Many people are pursued like that. A certain sister who lived in England was being harassed by the enemy. Every time she prayed, she would see her mother saying, "**You can run to wherever you want. I am your mother I will soon catch you.**" Every time she prayed about her problem, her mother would appear so she came home for deliverance. At the deliverance ground, when a prayer point was raised she heard the voice of her mother praying too behind her. When she looked back behold, it was her mother.

She came to Nigeria without letting anybody know and now the enemy she was running away from was sitting right at her back in the deliverance hall. She waited for the next prayer point and packed her bag and her Bible, ran away and came to look for me. She said, **"Sir, she followed me there. The person I have been dreaming about followed me to the place."** I asked her if she was sure she was seeing a human being or a spirit. She said, **"I did not confirm because immediately I heard the voice and looked, I ran away."** I told her to go back there the following day and if she found the woman, she should bring her to me. The following day, she did not see her again. So what she saw was the enemy, a destiny vulture pursuing her. That kind of person who was under a hot pursuit cannot settle down.

GOD'S BLUEPRINT

Everything that exists was designed in the mind of God before it came into being, so God is a God of destiny. Anything He created was with destiny and purpose. Everybody has a destiny in God.

I read the story of one man who saw the vision of God. According to him, he saw angels taking him round. He saw beautiful things. As they were showing him round, he found a rich man, a respectable man coming across the road and the angels treated the man with respect. He asked

Discovering God's PURPOSE

the angel, "Who is this big man coming?" The angel said, "Well that is the man you are supposed to be but you have refused to be what you are supposed to be. You are living a second hand life, collecting second hand miracles, and living in a second hand house," and the vision cleared from his eyes. Unfortunately, three days later, he died, never attaining that which was apportioned to him. That is why we need to pray the prayer of Joseph. Joseph prayed that, "**Lord, show me a vision of my destiny,**" and that was the origin of his problems. If he had kept quiet, he would have had no trouble. He saw a vision of his destiny and called a family meeting, and told them that he had a dream where he saw all of them bowing down to him. He saw that vision.

Christians are not supposed to be beggars or people to be pushed around because their Father is the owner of everything. But what can a Father do when He wants you in one place and you are somewhere else. Please take this prayer point: "**Oh God, show me a vision of my destiny, in the name of Jesus.**"

THE TRAGEDY

There is nothing more tragic than for a person to forfeit his or her divine destiny. A bird with broken wings cannot fly. It is a disaster to forfeit the purpose for which you were born into this world. No one else in this world is exactly like you. Your genetic make-up belongs only to you. Your fingerprints are personal to you and they are different from other fingerprints in the whole world. Likewise your destiny is unique. God had a hand in your life before the foundation of this world. But immediately the enemy takes somebody away from his place of destiny, he would be at the mercy of witches, wizards and other powers of darkness. If he cries for deliverance from God, He will say, **"My son or my daughter, what are you doing in that place?"** When Elijah was not in the place of his destiny, he prayed, **"Oh Lord God of Abraham, Isaac and Jacob, they have killed all your prophets. I only am left of your prophets and they seek my life to take it away. Kill me Oh God for I am not better than my fathers."** The Lord did not answer, He only said, **"What are you doing here Elijah?"** He was in the wrong place.

When you don't know your destiny, you live a wasted life. Unless there is a contest, there cannot be conquest. If you don't have a destiny to pursue, there will be nothing to fight for. If the enemies succeed in taking you far away from your destiny, you would be lost. I ministered to a lady during one of my travels abroad. She had five children who were all deaf and dumb. They smiled at me and I smiled at them. They were very playful but were not talking. The vulture has already dealt with them. Your destiny can only be fulfilled when it is intact.

DESTINY MANIPULATION

There is a department in the kingdom of darkness called the department of destiny manipulation. And when a person is manipulated out of his destiny, even prayers would be a hard work, and Bible reading would not be easy at all.

STRATEGIES OF DESTINY VULTURES

1. They have many strategies, but the major one is to make a person **ignorant of his personal destiny**. The Bible says that you shall know the truth and the truth shall make you free. It is the truth you know that shall set you free; the one you don't know cannot set you free. When a person is ignorant of his personal destiny, he would be living his life without a blueprint of his destiny. There is something called the blueprint of destiny. A good reader of the Bible would notice that whenever God has an assignment to do, He would call somebody and give him the blueprint. He called Moses to go and set His people free. He said to him, **"See that thou doest everything according to the pattern that I have shown to you."** He was telling Moses to follow the blueprint. Do you know the blueprint of your destiny? Who asked you to do the course of study you did in the university? Do you have the blueprint of your destiny?

Jesus said, "**The Son of man goeth as it is written of Him.**" Your blueprint is that thing that was written of you. It is the map of your life, plan, work, habitation, marriage, etc. If you don't have a blueprint or if your blueprint is wrong, the entire structure which you put upon that destiny will collapse. It is the correct blueprint that will give you purpose and direction. The prayer to know the blueprint of your destiny can take you five minutes, ten minutes, one hour, or one month. But it is a prayer that is worth praying. When you know the blueprint of your destiny, you cannot be discouraged or worried. When attacks come, you remain unmoved because you know you are going to a higher ground. When you have the blueprint, it will inspire you to a course of positive action. That map will chart your course in the journey of life.

Before a house is built, there must be a blueprint or a plan to show where everything would be fitted. Without a blueprint of that nature, you cannot build a good house. Once the blueprint of your destiny is not known or is lost or imprisoned or buried, it means that the vultures are at work. So, the first strategy of destiny vultures is to render a person ignorant of his personal destiny.

2. **Witchcraft manipulation:** They manipulate people out of their place of blessing and breakthroughs. They manipulate people out of the town or City of glory into where they become hewers of wood and drawers of water. This is happening on a daily basis.

3. **Delusion:** They send what the Bible calls delusion to people. It is the spirit that causes false belief and false opinion. It is a spirit that misleads people.

4. **They cast spell upon people:** Such people do the wrong things and go the wrong places.

5. They dispatch wicked spirits against the breakthrough of people. They dispatch wicked spirits against the destiny of people.

6. They sponsor negative pronouncements and confessions against people.

HOW DO YOU DELIVER YOURSELF FROM DESTINY VULTURES?

1. **You must be born-again,** if not destiny vultures will pursue you from the cradle to the grave.

2. **Pray to discover who you really are:** This is a very important prayer point.

3. **Pray for the revelation of your destiny blueprint.**

4. **Disconnect yourself from negative people:** that is, those that will not move your life forward. The Bible says that if you associate yourself with the wise, you will be wise, but when you are a companion of fools, you may not avoid harm's way.
5. **Watch your tongue.**
6. **Walk in holiness, honesty, and integrity.**

Just like the vulture is a patient bird, destiny manipulators can wait for a person to get old before they eventually finish the person up. It would be a disaster if you really don't know who you are because somebody else will tell you. When you don't know which direction you are going, somebody else will point to another direction to you, then servants would take up the horses of your life and the princes would be walking as servants. This calls for very serious prayers. It is time for the Holy Ghost to reschedule many people's lives. That business that has not moved your life forward, you should find out from the Lord whether you should be doing it. The house you have been living in that has not moved your life forward, it is time to know whether that is the place you should be in.

It is time to say, "**Oh Lord, I want to know the meaning of these destiny demotion dreams.**" It is time for you to analyze where you are, where you are going and what you will do to get there. You either know your blueprint or you don't know it, there is no middle road. There are people who

Discovering God's PURPOSE

are struggling and struggling with peanuts when the Lord has abundance for them. But what can you do when you cannot see the abundance? There are some who are blindly stuck to what will not make them comfortable. You need to be detached and relocated to your place of prosperity.

Some people are 2000, 3000 miles away from their destiny. Many have already made terrible mistakes. Some people have been committing consistent errors for the past twenty-five years and because of that, they are out of their pattern of destiny. They need to do some prayers to get back in line to where God wants them to be. Some have built their houses in the wrong places and the spirits of the land are fighting them. These are things that we need to address.

PRAYER POINTS
1. Destiny vulture, vomit my destiny, in Jesus' name.
2. Visions of my divine destiny, come upon my life, in the name of Jesus.
3. Every career or business that will not prosper my life, be disconnected, in the name of Jesus.
4. The enemy will not determine my destiny, in the name of Jesus.
5. Every witchcraft servant riding on the horse of my destiny, come down, in the name of Jesus.
6. Every evil destiny pattern, die, in the name of Jesus.

7. Wherever I missed my way in the journey of life, my Father, help me, in Jesus' name.
8. Every family destiny cage, what are you waiting for? Die, in the name of Jesus.
9. Every spiritual bastard, pursuing my destiny, die in the name of Jesus.
10. Every job that will not move me forward, change by fire, in the name of Jesus.
11. Where is the Lord God of Elijah? Arise, promote my destiny, in the name of Jesus.
12. Every spiritual relative stealing from me, scatter, in the name of Jesus.
13. Every curse issued against my destiny, backfire, in the name of Jesus.
14. Power to reach my goal, fall upon my life, in the name of Jesus.
15. Every witchcraft embargo on my finances, die, in the name of Jesus.
16. Every witchcraft embargo on my career/business/job, die in the name of Jesus.
17. Every witchcraft embargo on my marriage, die, in the name of Jesus.
18. Anointing for turnaround breakthrough, come upon my life, in the name of Jesus.
19. My Father, reveal the blueprint of my destiny to me, in the name of Jesus.

CHAPTER 4

When You WIN

What a tragedy it is, to go to the cemetery and find out that the dead that is being buried, and the person conducting the burial are candidates for hell fire. It is a tragedy for someone that has access to the banquet hall, that sees all the goodies set on the table, but when it is time to feast, he is turned out, and asked to leave.

Many people have access to the kingdom of God but will not be allowed in because of the sins that easily beset them. For some, it is fornication or adultery, lying, anger, worrying etc., these tendencies will not allow them to gain entrance into the kingdom of God.

Do you earnestly contend for that kingdom? Are you a good example of righteousness? Are you attracting people to the Lord Jesus Christ?

There was a man who went to England for his Ph.D at the age of 36. I was always telling him about Jesus but he refused to get serious with the Lord. He spent 8 years on a 3 - year course and on the day he was to defend his thesis, he fumbled and for four hours he was before the panel. In the end, the examiner declared that he was not the one that wrote the thesis. On that day, he could not answer any question correctly. He could not even remember the title of his thesis. When he came out, I told him that he needed to fight, spiritual warfare, against the powers that were determined to hinder him. He told me that it was all superstition. I kept quite. This man spent two more years before he got the degree.

When you are under God's security and you are contending against the enemy, God too will fight for you. However, if you are a par-time contender, He will not take you seriously. When you contend only if you are happy, only when you are praised, only when your contract goes through, then you are not serious. Nobody will enlist a part-time soldier to go to the war front when there is a full-time soldier who is able and ready to go.

Our life is supposed to advertise the glory of God and His power. Our life is supposed to confound and astonish the enemy and let them know what stuff we are made of. Many people are against MFM, many are against Dr. Olukoya but the more the enemy rages, the more the Lord is blessing the ministry. We have to astonish our enemies, by earnestly contending for the faith that was once delivered unto the saints.

WHEN GOD FIGHTS FOR YOU

What I am saying in essence, is that if you have decided to serve the Lord Jesus Christ and you have left the world and the beggarly powers, why not go totally out for Him? Release yourself to Him and he will take you up with both arms and you cannot fail. In that same university as that man mentioned earlier, I went in for the defense of my thesis and within 25 minutes, I had finished and bagged my degree and I was congratulated.

Our warfare with the enemy is not a plaything. You cannot organise a peaceful rally against the enemy. You have to be sure of what you are doing. We are fighting against terrible, unseen spirits, great evil princes, large number of terrible spirits, principalities, powers, rulers of darkness, masterminds, executives, remote controlling powers, evil powers, strongmen, strongholds, evil craftiness and evil devices, evil council, etc.

The question is, how well are you fighting the battle? Are you doing very well?

Are you one of those the Lord is telling they are not serious? Have you ever had a dream in which someone snatched your Bible from you? Do you see yourself naked in the dream? Do you see yourself in the dream arriving at church when the service has come to a close? Do you see yourself in the dream called upon to preach and your voice suddenly disappears? Do you see yourself in a toilet standing in faeces or standing on a dunghill? What I am saying now concerns everybody no matter what post you are holding. If Jesus comes now to evaluate what you have done or are doing and the motive for doing it, will He say:

"Well done, faithful and obedient servant?" Will He say that you have successfully contended for the faith? Are you just thinking about the miracles you need - husband, wealth, healing?

HIGH STAKES

The stakes are very high and what I am saying, transcends this planet and goes to eternity. Since it is an eternity affair, you should think about it. Human beings sometimes do not know their priorities; they chase shadows.

REASONS FOR FAILURE

Why are people unable to contend for the kingdom?

1. **Spiritual Laziness.** Laziness in the life of a soldier results in disaster and all kinds of things. A man was employed as security guard and one night, he was asleep when he heard a screechy noise. Instead of getting up to investigate, he asked who it was and there was no reply. He threw a stone in that direction and all he heard was the sound of the stone hitting something and resumed sleep. The following morning, he found out that the machine he was supposed to be guarding had been detached and the engine stolen.

Laziness can defeat a person, a business, a fellowship, it can defeat a whole race. That demon whispering **"tomorrow"** into your ears is a friend to your enemy; it is the same demon that says **"later."** You made up your mind in January to read through the Bible and by September, you have not finished two books, laziness is at work. It is the one that tells you to get angry and rain abuse on the person opposing you even though you hear the still small voice in the background counseling you to take it easy. Lazy people are the ones that easily get angry. Procrastination is a child of laziness, a lazy man may not even start a project at all. He could have very good ideas but will never do anything to get them moving. A lazy person will do things halfway and not finish, he would abandon a project to start a new one. He will never agree that he is lazy. Many of us need to pray that the spirit of laziness should depart from our lives and then invite the zeal of the Lord to take over.

We need the holy fire of God's zeal upon our lives. Nobody can be lazy and amount to anything. The enemy has adopted this tactic to slow people down. **"Contend for the faith, which was once delivered to the saints"**. There is a satanic prayer against many, there is a satanic purpose against many people. Some have satanic challenges, some are suffering from satanic decrees and satanic reinforcement, satanic intelligence. Such people should give themselves to the Lord today. Lose yourself in Him completely, let Him have the totality of your being and you will see what He will do for you. There is victory for all believers.

> *Nay, in all these things, we are more than conquerors through Him that loved us —* Romans 8-37.

There is victory for all believers and for us to have the victory and contend for the kingdom, these things we must do:

2. **Total Submission.** It means giving oneself to God in full and complete surrender, yielding to what God wants you to do. It may not be convenient, it may be uncomfortable but you have to yield to the Master. Any part of you that is not surrendered to God, can be used by the devil to bring you into bondage. So hand over your possessions to God, your plan, purpose, money, time, abilities, friendship, your past, present, future, everything. Hand them over to God. Before God can make great use of you, you must completely submit to Him. Submit your heart, your speech, your temper, everything. Anyone who wants to have his own way will not be able to contend for the faith that

was once delivered to the saints. All these traits in us that will always want us to have things done our own way must be drained out of us. Some people are not happy when they are not allowed to do things their own way. All the harshness, severity, criticism, must be drained out of our lives. The ability to sing, preach, win souls, write tracts or other activities, do not replace submission to God, attending a Bible college does not replace submission to God.

Far you to successfully contend for the faith that was once delivered the saints, God must conquer you.

Do not be like the man who pestered God to use him and the Lord said he had to die to flesh first. As God was going to kill flesh in him and bury it, the man had a hammer in his hand. As soon as God put him in a coffin and turned back, the man tore open the lid of the coffin with the hammer in his hand, and came out.

There are some people who say that they are changing gradually instead of yielding self to complete death. When you are not totally yielded, God will not be able to do His work in your life, He will not be able to work His miracles in your life. When you are totally submissive to God, you will no longer seek to please yourself but God. Then, everyone will be on fire for the Almighty and be working towards the will of God for their lives. A lot of people spend the major portion of their lives chasing shadows. What a pity for someone who gets born-again at the age of 60 and is still not be able to discern between right and wrong.

> *But if we walk in the light, as He is in the light, we have fellowship one with another, and the Blood of Jesus Christ His son, cleanseth his from all sin. If we say that we have no sin, we deceive ourselves if we confess our sins, He is faithful and just to cleanse us from all unrighteousness* — 1John 1:7-9.

This means we must be willing to have all our sins cleansed. We should not harbour little sins. Real victory, belongs to those who are willing to have all their sins removed from their lives. If you confess your sins, God is ready not only to forgive, but to cleanse such sins including fear, doubt, shyness to testify to what God has done for you, resentment, unwillingness to give, coldness of heart, selfishness, etc. You should ask God to cleanse you. If a Christian attends a Bible - believing church and hears the word of God regularly, pray fire prayers like we do in MFM, but in spite of this, still commits fornication, adultery, stealing etc, there is only one explanation: the person is a child of perdition; the person just decided to perish and there is nothing anyone can do to help him since it is a personal decision.

3. **Be filled with the Holy Spirit.** It is a sin to refuse to be filled with the Holy Spirit and it is also a sin to refuse to accord the Holy Spirit the right to full control of one's being. A person is as holy only as far as the Holy Spirit fills him or her with His holiness .When the Holy Spirit enters into your life, He enters into every part of your life and the anointing comes upon you, you become a new person. Elisha was so anointed, that even after his death, his bones carried life. If you want God's presence, then lose your own presence. Even Moses of the Old Testament, was not satisfied with what he had. He wanted more of the Lord. Have you received the baptism of the Holy Spirit? Then, press for more infilling; maybe you only speak in tongues, press for more infilling. May be you are the kind that gets to church services late; because you have a job that takes your time; you had better change your mind and be serious with God.

4. **Be occupied for the Lord.** Get yourself busy in the vineyard of the Lord. That servant that thought he was not good enough was sent to hellfire. Find out about the things you can do for the Lord. Do not be an idle pair of hands which is a ready tool in the hands

of the devil. God is not under any obligation to bless those who refuse to word for Him. He does not want those who only seek His hand and not His face.

5. **Have genuine love.** You must have a sound intention to love others. Love in the Bible means that you are prepared to help another person no matter what it costs you. Love is the mark of Christianity. It is an attitude which never feels superior; it is devoid of criticism and deeply concerned by the good of the other people. Sometimes, it can be painful. Jesus Himself is an example of this - He wore a crown of thorns, the agony of nails, becoming sin for us, bearing our infirmities, being forsaken and eventually dying for us.

- How many people do you pray for?
- How many needy people do you care for?
- Do you know the names of brethren?
- Do you greet people beside you?

When there is no love, you cannot really contend for the faith, which was once delivered to the saints.

Beloved, I would like you to ask yourself if you are really contending for the faith. Are you serving the Lord? Can sufficient evidence be adduced to show you're really serving Him? Can you be accused of serving the Lord for what you could get from Him? You know yourself, what is your mark before the Almighty?

Can the devil accuse you of troubling him? Have you turned to a commercial prophet? Do you use your talents and gifts for the Lord? Search your heart. Jesus is looking for those whose hearts are right with Him. Is ours right with Him? What do you weigh in the balance of the Almighty? What are you going to do about it? The righteousness of yesterday is not sufficient for today.

At this juncture, I want you to talk to the Lord. Ask Him to cleanse you with His Blood and to forgive you where you have gone wrong.

If however you are not yet born-again, I would advise that you surrender your life to the Lord Jesus Christ now. He is right there with you and is ready to hear you as you call. Confess your sins to Him, name them one by one and ask Him to forgive you and cleanse you from all unrighteousness. Claim the redemptive power in the Blood of Jesus that was shed on the cross at Calvary for the remission of your sins.

Renounce the world and the devil; be sure you will not go back to the devil; be sure you will not go back to them again.

Discovering God's PURPOSE

I congratulate you for this decision that you have just taken.

I pray that it shall be permanent in your life and the kingdom of God will be established in your life in the Name of Jesus.

Now take these prayer points with determination in your heart:-

1. Holy Ghost, crown my head and life with divine glory, in the name of Jesus.

2. Any tongue, speaking against me, when I am being considered by my partner, be silenced now, in the name of Jesus.

3. I declare that I shall not miss my season of marriage, in the name of Jesus.

4. I prophesy that I am the delight of my partner, in the name of Jesus.

5. Holy Ghost, shut the mouth of anyone speaking against me now; in the name of Jesus.

6. I prophesy that my courtship will lead to marriage and I shall be fruitful, in the name of Jesus.

7. I close any door that I have opened to the devil through my confessions and past actions, in Jesus' name.

8. Lord Jesus, wash me from the impurity and stigma of the past, in the name of Jesus.

9. You gates and everlasting doors, resisting my marital breakthrough, be lifted and be uprooted, in the name of Jesus.

10. I lay hold on my covenant right of marriage, therefore, I shall be happily married, in the name of Jesus.

11. Every household enemy, resisting my breakthroughs, fall down and die, in the name of Jesus.

12. Every unfriendly friend, delegated against my blessing, scatter, in the name of Jesus.

13. Every spirit of disobedience and rebellion in my life, die, in the name of Jesus.

14. Every demon propagating satanic covenants in my life, fall down and die, in the name of Jesus.

15. Begin to thank God for answering your prayers.

Others Books Published by Dr. D. K. Olukoya

1. 20 Marching Orders To Fulfill Your Destiny
2. 30 Prophetic Arrows From Heaven
3. 30 Things The Anointing Can Do For You
4. Abraham's Children in Bondage
5. A-Z of Complete Deliverance
6. Basic Prayer Patterns
7. Be Prepared
8. Bewitchment must Die
9. Biblical Principles of Dream Interpretation
10. Born Great, But Tied Down
11. Breaking Bad Habits
12. Breakthrough Prayers For Business Professionals
13. Bringing Down The Power of God
14. Brokenness
15. Can God Trust You?
16. Command The Morning
17. Connecting to The God of Breakthroughs
18. Consecration Commitment & Loyalty
19. Contending For The Kingdom
20. Criminals In The House Of God
21. Dancers At The Gate of Death
22. Dealing Destiny Vultures
23. Dealing With Destiny Thieves
24. Dealing With Hidden Curses
25. Dealing With Local Satanic Technology
26. Dealing With Satanic Exchange
27. Dealing With The Evil Powers Of Your Father's House

Others Books Published by Dr. D. K. Olukoya

28. Dealing With Tropical Demons
29. Dealing With Unprofitable Roots
30. Dealing With Witchcraft Barbers
31. Deep Secrets, Deep Deliverance
32. Deliverance By Fire
33. Deliverance From Evil Foundation
34. Deliverance From Spirit Husband And Spirit Wife
35. Deliverance From Multiple Bondage
36. Deliverance From The Limiting Powers
37. Deliverance of The Brain
38. Deliverance Of The Conscience
39. Deliverance Of The Head
40. Deliverance of The Tongue
41. Deliverance: God's Medicine Bottle
42. Destiny Clinic
43. Destroying Satanic Masks
44. Discovering God's Purpose
45. Disgracing Soul Hunters
46. Divine Military Training
47. Divine Prescription For Your Total Immunity
48. Divine Yellow Card
49. Dominion Prosperity
50. Drawers Of Power From The Heavenlies
51. Evil Appetite
52. Evil Umbrella
53. Facing Both Ways
54. Failure In The School Of Prayer

Others Books Published by Dr. D. K. Olukoya

55. Fire For Life's Journey
56. For We Wrestle ...
57. Freedom Indeed
58. God's Key To A Happy Life
59. Healing Through Prayers
60. Holiness Unto The Lord
61. Holy Cry
62. Holy Fever
63. Hour Of Decision
64. How To Obtain Personal Deliverance
65. How To Pray When Surrounded By The Enemies
66. I Am Moving Forward
67. Idols Of The Heart
68. Igniting Your Inner Fire
69. Is This What They Died For?
70. Kill Your Goliath By Fire
71. Killing The Serpent of Frustration
72. Let Fire Fall
73. Let God Answer By Fire
74. Limiting God
75. Lord, Behold Their Threatening
76. Madness of The Heart
77. Making Your Way Through The Traffic Jam of Life
78. Meat For Champions
79. Medicine For Winners
80. My Burden For The Church
81. My Enemies will not Rejoice Over Me

Others Books Published by Dr. D. K. Olukoya

82. Open Heavens Through Holy Disturbance
83. Overpowering Witchcraft
84. Paralysing The Riders And The Horse
85. Personal Spiritual Check-Up
86. Possessing The Tongue of Fire
87. Power Against Coffin Spirits
88. Power Against Destiny Quenchers
89. Power Against Dream Criminals
90. Power Against Local Wickedness
91. Power Against Marine Spirits
92. Power Against Spiritual Terrorists
93. Power Against The Mystery of Wickedness
94. Power Against Unclean Spirits
95. Power Must Change Hands
96. Power of Brokenness
97. Power To Disgrace The Oppressors
98. Power To Put The Enemy To Shame
99. Power To Recover Your Birthright
100. Power To Recover Your Lost Glory
101. Power To Shut Satanic Doors
102. Pray Your Way To Breakthroughs
103. Prayer Strategies For Singles
104. Prayer Is The Battle
105. Prayer Rain
106. Prayer To Kill Enchantment
107. Prayer To Make You Fulfill Your Divine Destiny
108. Prayer Warfare Against 70 Mad Spirits

Others Books Published by Dr. D. K. Olukoya

109. Prayers For Open Heavens
110. Prayers To Destroy Diseases And Infirmities
111. Prayers To Move From Minimum To Maximum
112. Praying Against Foundational Poverty
113. Praying Against The Spirit Of The Valley
114. Praying In The Storm
115. Praying To Destroy Satanic Roadblocks
116. Praying To Dismantle Witchcraft
117. Principles of Conclusive Prayers
118. Principles Of Prayer
119. Raiding The House of The Strongman
120. Release From Destructive Covenants
121. Revoking Evil Decrees
122. Safeguarding Your Home
123. Satanic Diversion Of The Black Race
124. Secrets of Spiritual Growth And Maturity
125. Setting The Covens Ablaze
126. Seventy Rules of Spiritual Warfare
127. Seventy Sermons To Preach To Your Destiny
128. Silencing The Birds Of Darkness
129. Slave Masters
130. Slaves Who Love Their Chains
131. Smite The Enemy And He Will Flee
132. Speaking Destruction Unto The Dark Rivers
133. Spiritual Education
134. Spiritual Growth And Maturity
135. Spiritual Warfare And The Home

Others Books Published by Dr. D. K. Olukoya

136. Stop Them Before They Stop You
137. Strategic Praying
138. Strategy Of Warfare Praying
139. Students In The School Of Fear
140. Symptoms Of Witchcraft Attack
141. Taking The Battle To The Enemy's Gate
142. The Amazing Power of Faith
143. The Baptism of Fire
144. The Battle Against The Spirit Of Impossibility
145. The Chain Breaker
146. The Deep Truth About Marriage
147. The Dinning Table Of Darkness
148. The Enemy Has Done This
149. The Evil Cry Of Your Family Idol
150. The Fire Of Revival
151. The Gateway To Spiritual Power
152. The Great Deliverance
153. The Hidden Viper
154. The Internal Stumbling Block
155. The Lord is A Man of War
156. The Mystery Of Mobile Curses
157. The Mystery Of The Mobile Temple
158. The Power of Aggressive Prayer Warriors
159. The Power of Priority
160. The Prayer Eagle
161. The Pursuit Of Success
162. The Scale of The Almighty

Others Books Published by Dr. D. K. Olukoya

163. The School of Tribulation
164. The Seasons Of Life
165. The Secrets Of Greatness
166. The Serpentine Enemies
167. The Skeleton In Your Grandfather's Cupboard
168. The Slow Learners
169. The Snake In The Power House
170. The Spirit Of The Crab
171. The Star Hunters
172. The Star In Your Sky
173. The Terrible Agenda
174. The Tongue Trap
175. The Unconquerable Power
176. The University of Champions
177. The Unlimited God
178. The Vagabond Spirit
179. The Way Of Divine Encounter
180. The Wealth Transfer Agenda
181. Tied Down In The Spirits
182. Too Hot To Handle
183. Turnaround Breakthrough
184. Unprofitable Foundations
185. Victory Over Death
186. Victory Over Satanic Dreams
187. Victory Over Your Greatest Enemies
188. Violent Prayers Against Stubborn Situations
189. War At The Edge Of Breakthroughs

Others Books Published by Dr. D. K. Olukoya

190. Wasted At The Market Square of Life
191. Wasting The Wasters
192. Ways To Provoke Divine Vengeance
193. Wealth Must Change Hands
194. What You Must Know About The House Fellowship
195. When God Is Silent
196. When The Battle is from Home
197. When The Deliverer Need Deliverance
198. When The Enemy Hides
199. When The Enemy Is On The Rampage
200. When Things Get Hard
201. When You Are Knocked Down
202. When You Are Under Attack
203. When You Need A Change
204. Where Is Your Faith?
205. While Men Slept
206. Woman! Thou Art Loosed.
207. Your Battle And Your Strategy
208. Your Foundation And Destiny
209. Your Mouth And Your Deliverance
210. Your Mouth And Your Warfare

YORUBA PUBLICATIONS

1. Adura Agbayori
2. Adura Ti Nsi Oke Ni'di
3. Ojo Adura

Others Books Published by Dr. D. K. Olukoya

FRENCH PUBLICATIONS

1. Bilan Spirituel Personnel
2. Cantique Des Contiques
3. Commander Le Matin
4. Comment Recevior La Delivrance Du Mari Et Femme De Nuit
5. Comment Se Delivrer Soi-meme
6. Demanteler La Sorcellerie
7. En Finir Avec Les Forces Malefiques De La Maison De Ton Pere
8. Espirit De Vagabondage
9. Femme Tu Es Liberee
10. Frappez l'adversaire Et Il Fuira
11. L'etoile Dans Votre Ciel
12. La Deliverance De La Tete
13. La Deliverance: Le Flacon De Medicament Dieu
14. La Deviation Satanique De La Race Noire
15. Le Combat Spirituel Et Le Foyer
16. Le Mauvais Cri Des Idoles
17. Le Programme De Tranfert De Richesse
18. Les Etudiants A l'ecole De La Peur
19. Les Saisons De La Vie
20. Les Strategies De Prieres Pour Les Celibataires
21. Ne Grand Mais Lie
22. Pluie De Priere
23. Pouvoir Contre Les Demond Tropicaux
24. Povoir Contre Les Terrorites Spirituel
25. Prier Jusqu'a Remporter La Victoire
26. Priere De Percees Pour Les Hommes D'affaires

Others Books Published by Dr. D. K. Olukoya

27. Priere Pour Detruire Les Maladies Et Infirmites
28. Prieres Violentes Pour Humilier Les Problemes Opiniatres
29. Prieres De Comat Contre 70 Espirits Dechanines
30. Quand Les Choses Deviennent Difficiles
31. Que l'envoutement Perisse
32. Revoquer Les Decrets Malefiques
33. Se Liberer Des Alliances Malefiques
34. Ton Combat Et Ta Strategie
35. Victoires Sur Les Reves Sataniques
36. Votre Fondement Et Votre Destin

ANNUAL 70 DAYS PRAYER AND FASTING PUBLICATIONS

1. Prayers That Bring Miracles
2. Let God Answer By Fire
3. Prayers To Mount With Wings As Eagles
4. Prayers That Bring Explosive Increase
5. Prayers For Open Heavens
6. Prayers To Make You Fulfill Your Divine Destiny
7. Prayers That Make God To Answer And Fight By Fire
8. Prayers That Bring Unchallengeable Victory And Breakthrough Rainfall Bombardments
9. Prayers That Bring Dominion Prosperity And Uncommon Success
10. Prayers That Bring Power And Overflowing Progress
11. Prayers That Bring Laughter And Enlargement Breakthroughs

Others Books Published by Dr. D. K. Olukoya

12. Prayers That Bring Uncommon Favour And Breakthroughs
13. Prayers That Bring Unprecedented Greatness And Unmatchable Increase
14. Prayers That Bring Awesome Testimonies And Turn Around Breakthroughs
15. Prayers That Bring Glorious Restoration
16. Prayers That Bring Unrivaled Lifting
17. Prayers That Bring Dominion Celebration And Supernatural Open Doors

Books Published by Pastor (Mrs.) Shade Olukoya

1. Daughters of Philip
2. I Decree An Uncommon Change
3. Power To Fulfil Your Destiny
4. Principles of A Successful Marriage
5. The Call of God
6. When Your Destiny Is Under Attack
7. Woman of Wonder
8. Violence Against Negative Voices

**The Books, Tapes and CDs (Audio and Video)
All Obtainable At:**

1. Battle Cry Christian Ministries
   322, Herbert Macaulay Way, Sabo, Yaba, Lagos
   Phone: 01 8044415, 0803 304 4239

2. MFM International Bookshop
   13, Olasimbo Street, Onike, Yaba, Lagos

3. MFM Prayer City
   Km 12, Lagos/Ibadan Expressway

4. Battle Cry Christian Ministries
   Abuja Zonal Office & Bookshop
   4, Nasarawa Street,
   Block A, Shop 4, Garki, Old Market
   Phone: 0813 586 5868, 0815 910 3039

5. 54, Akeju Street, off Shipeolu Street
   Palmgrove, Lagos

6. All MFM Churches Nationwide

7. All Leading Christian Bookstores

BOOK ORDER

Is there any book written by Dr. D. K. Olukoya
(General Overseer MFM Ministries)
that you would like to have?
Have you seen his latest books?
To place an order for this End-Time Materials,
Call : 08161229775

Battle Cry Christian Ministries... equipping the saints of God
God bless you.

The Book

God has a purpose for you like any other person. The question is, how do you know God's purpose for your life? This is what this book is all about.

In Ecclesiastes 10 verse 7, the scripture tells of how destinies can be changed. This is why chapter three of this book demands a good study and understanding. It gives you details on the scales on your eyes that may not allow you to know your destiny, how to be aware of spiritual vultures out to eat up destinies. You are given six destiny vultures, then six ways by which you can deliver yourself from them.

If you agree that you have a very high stake that transcends this planet and goes to eternity, you are given five clues on how to achieve this.

About BCCM, MFM Ministries and the Author

Dr. Daniel Kolawole Olukoya is the General Overseer of the Battle Cry Christian Ministries and Mountain of Fire and Miracles Ministries. The Mountain of Fire and Miracles Ministries' Headquarters in Lagos, Nigeria is the largest single Christian congregation in Africa with attendance of over 120,000 in single meetings.

MFM is a full gospel ministry devoted to the revival of Apostolic signs, Holy Ghost fireworks, miracles and the unlimited demonstration of the power of God to deliver to the uttermost. Absolute holiness within and without as the greatest spiritual insecticide and a pre-requisite for heaven is openly taught. MFM is a do-it-yourself gospel ministry, where your hands are trained to wage war and your fingers to do battle.

Dr. Olukoya holds a first class honours degree in Microbiology from the University of Lagos, Nigeria and a PhD in Molecular Genetics from the University of Reading, United Kingdom. As a researcher, he has over seventy scientific publications to his credit.

Anointed by God, Dr. D. K. Olukoya is a prophet, evangelist, teacher and preacher of the Word. His life and that of his wife, Shade and their son, Elijah Toluwani are living proofs that all power belongs to God.

The Battle Cry Christian Ministries is devoted to:
(a) teaching and disseminating information on Christian spiritual warfare,
(b) making available life-changing Christian articles and books at affordable prices and
(c) preparing an army of aggressive prayer warriors and intercessors in this end-time.

Published by:

The Battle Cry Christian Ministries
ISBN : 978-978-920-053-5

www.ingramcontent.com/pod-product-compliance
Lightning Source LLC
Chambersburg PA
CBHW060853050426
42453CB00008B/963